THE 🐈 LITTLE
KITTEN
Book

ELIZABETH MARTYN
DAVID TAYLOR

Photography by Jane Burton

DORLING KINDERSLEY, INC.
New York

A DORLING KINDERSLEY BOOK

EDITOR *Jane Mason*

ART EDITOR *Lee Griffiths*

MANAGING EDITOR *Krystyna Mayer*

MANAGING ART EDITOR *Derek Coombes*

PRODUCTION *Hilary Stephens*

First American Edition, 1991
10 9 8 7 6 5 4 3 2 1

Dorling Kindersley, Inc., 232 Madison Avenue
New York, New York 10016

ISBN 1-879431-61-0
Library of Congress Catalog Card Number 91-072734

Reproduced by Colourscan, Singapore
Printed and bound in Hong Kong by Imago

CONTENTS

FROM
Kitten
TO CAT

An adorable kitten will grow up quickly to become the wise and wonderful feline who shares your life.

EARLY DAYS

When a mother cat has given birth to her kittens, and washed each one thoroughly, she should be given a warm, refreshing drink and offered food. She may refuse both food and drink for a few hours, being reluctant to leave her young. A clean litter box should also be within reach. While she is feeding her kittens, the mother will need three times her usual intake of food and must be given extra meals every day until the kittens are weaned.

THE FAMILY UNIT
Mother and babies need to be kept in a well-heated room.
It is a good idea to ask the vet to check in during the first
24 hours to see that all is well with mother and offspring.
The kittens should suckle readily from the first hours of life
and, to start with, will feed every two hours.

Just 12 Hours Old

Newborn kittens stay close to their mother because they are blind and unable to walk. Once the kittens begin crawling away from the nest, they have to find their way back using their sense of smell or by calling for their mother to fetch them. Their sensitive whiskers warn them of any obstacles. Everyone will want to admire the newborns, but it is better to discourage visitors for the first weeks.

Four Days Old

Kittens utter their first purrs when feeding. By the end of the week, their birth weight has doubled. When they are not suckling, kittens sleep, curled up closely against their mother and each other. Tiny kittens will hiss when strange scents come into range.

GROWING UP

In the second week after birth, dramatic events occur. Hearing and sight develop to match the kittens' excellent sense of smell. Little milk teeth appear and the kittens' weight gain is rapid. When only a month old, kittens begin to wash themselves and each other, rather than being groomed by their mother. They start to explore and are soon clambering into every corner.

*T*EN DAYS OLD
The kittens' eyes open and their ears, which have been folded over, begin to perk up.

Three Weeks Old

At three weeks it is time to start walking, although the kittens may be unsteady at first. Little Ginger still calls to her mother for help when she wanders too far.

Five Weeks Old

Kittens can start on solid food now: fresh meat, or fish, or canned food. Small meals should be served, always at room temperature.

ADOLESCENCE

Kittens should not be parted from their mother until they are at least eight weeks old, when they will be fully weaned. At six weeks old, they become used to human company, do not object to being handled, and are not distressed if they are moved away from their mother. At two months, kittens should have their first vaccinations, followed by a booster a few weeks later.

Four Months Old

Ginger can now rear up and balance
on her hind legs. All the kittens'
senses are completely developed now
and their movements are well-
controlled and agile. Females should
be neutered at four to six months,
males at six months.

Six Months Old

Kittens can be allowed to venture
out of doors. They love exploring
and will mark out their territories to
warn off other cats. Although still
playful, kittens slowly lose the total
exuberance of kittenhood and
become calmer and less boisterous.

Two Months Old

All the milk teeth are
through now, and the
kittens can be fed entirely
on solid foods, two or
three meals daily. Mother
and kittens remain very
close and behave
affectionately toward
each other. Kittens from
the same litter continue to
play together but gradually
lose some of the intimate
closeness of babyhood.

GALLERY OF
Kittens

*A magnificent multitude
of irresistible kittens –
consummate characters,
charmers, athletes,
and hunters in action
and at rest.*

KITTENS OF CHARACTER

Kittens have a knack for keeping their owners entertained for hours on end with a constantly changing display of kittenish demeanor ranging from sleepy to active, fierce to adoring. Indeed, as a notorious cat-lover once remarked, "a kitten is much more amusing than half the people one is obliged to live with."

Serious kitten

Chatty kitten

Sleepy kitten

Pensive kitten

Watchful kitten

Curious kitten

Innocent kitten

Timid kitten

PLAYING TOGETHER

From a few weeks old, kittens play together, staging mock fights that appear ferociously realistic to the onlooker. The kittens leap on each other, biting and clawing, yet no one ever gets hurt. Young cats have a built-in control mechanism to ensure that their battles never get out of hand. They quickly learn to defend their territory, either by fighting or by using body language to intimidate their opponent.

POUNCING PRACTICE
Every kitten learns to creep up on prey and get poised for the final spring. A cat also crouches very low with ears laid back to show submission.

CATERISTICS

Crafty kittens fight on their backs, leaving paws and teeth free for combat

Even the fiercest boxing matches never draw blood

Fluffed-up fur stands away from the body to intimidate the attacker

BALANCING ACT

Tiny kittens rear up unsteadily on their hind legs. Once they stop tumbling over, they can learn the techniques adult cats use to catch birds and mice.

PLAYING WITH TOYS

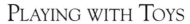

Kittens treat almost any object as a toy, as long as they can chase it, roll it along the floor, jump on it, or hide underneath it. These are the movements they will use in adulthood when hunting their prey. Kittens stalk their toys, pounce on them, hook them out of inaccessible corners, and carry them off triumphantly, just as they would treat a live mouse or bird. Primitive survival instincts lie behind such innocent tricks and games.

ALL IN A TANGLE
Soft toys that can be firmly gripped with teeth and claws provide lots of fun for a boisterous ginger whirlwind who loves helping her owner to knit!

Hide-and-seek

An old piece of blanket makes a fine camouflage for a Tonkinese trickster intent upon surprising one of her siblings. Most cats enjoy hiding themselves away where they think no one can see them and then leaping out at unwary passers-by.

Cateristics

Anything that moves, makes a noise, or can be tossed in the air is fair game to a kitten

Toys dangled or swung on a string by teasing owners always attract a kitten's attention

Rival kittens will steal each others' playthings to establish who is boss cat

Fighting and Wrestling

Danger, kittens at play! Humans who get caught up in a feline battleground are liable to find their legs being scaled as escape routes or their heads being used as launch pads. But although this type of behavior may look serious, like many kitten games, its real purpose is to provide a practice run in the art of self-defense. The players always emerge unscathed, and, if raised together, may well continue their friendly scrapping into adulthood.

Rough Stuff
Tiny warriors fluff out their fur to make themselves look as huge and fierce as possible.

GOTCHA!
Tortoiseshell and tabby enjoy a rough-and-tumble.

CATERISTICS

❧

Keep glass and china far away from battlegrounds

❧

Hissing and spitting accompany exciting games

❧

Boredom often strikes in mid-fight

CLIMBING AND CHASING

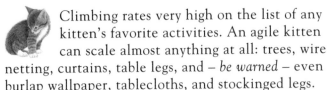

Climbing rates very high on the list of any kitten's favorite activities. An agile kitten can scale almost anything at all: trees, wire netting, curtains, table legs, and – *be warned* – even burlap wallpaper, tablecloths, and stockinged legs. The feline eye is attracted by any tiny movement that could mean food. That's why a playful kitten will give chase to a falling leaf, a snowflake, a beam of light, a shadow, or a trailing shoelace. It's all part of the finely honed hunting instinct.

TEMPTING TAIL

Pouncing on the unguarded tail of another kitten is great sport. Failing that, all cats love to chase their own tails, often whirling round and round dizzily in pursuit of the elusive bait.

O<small>H</small> D<small>EAR</small>!
*All cats occasionally slip
up, but they usually land
on all four paws.*

C<small>ATERISTICS</small>

*The more inaccessible
the perch, the greater
the challenge*

*Chasing is one of life's
little pleasures*

*Determination can get a
kitten almost anywhere*

LEARNING TO HUNT

The urge to pursue prey is an instinct deeply ingrained in the cat's nature – to the distress of many owners. Although some cats seem much less interested than others, there's little you can do to deter your cat totally from exercising what is, after all, a very natural impulse. A mother cat who does not enjoy hunting is likely to have similar kittens.

CAUGHT IN THE ACT
After the first pounce, cats may play with their prey for some time before killing it.

CATERISTICS

Dramatic leaps are powered by strong back and leg muscles

By stalking each other, kittens learn how to use stealth and surprise in the hunt

At ten weeks old, kittens have developed balance and grace

HIGH JUMP

Cats make a high, leaping pounce when they want to catch birds. Some cats never learn to do this, and consequently only catch fledglings who are too young to fly away from danger.

PLAYTIME PREY

A kitten will toss a catnip mouse or other small toy in the air, catching it between her paws and nibbling at it, just as she would a real mouse.

KEEPING CLEAN

Until they are about four weeks old, the mother cat grooms the kittens. After that, they begin to wash themselves, and by six weeks will be doing a very thorough job. Cats have rough tongues that act like miniature brushes as they lick themselves all over. Not only does personal grooming keep the fur clean and smooth, removing any loose hair or dirt; this practice also helps to reinforce the cat's own body scent.

*T*EAM *W*ORK
Kittens often wash each other vigorously. The purpose is not so much to keep each other neat and tidy, as to show their affection and reinforce bonds within the litter.

FACE FACTS

Cats use their paws as "wash mitts" to keep their faces and tricky areas behind the ears clean. The paw is first washed, then licked repeatedly and rubbed firmly over the face and around the ears until the cat is satisfied.

NEAT BIB

This kitten is using her right paw to steady herself as she carefully grooms her abdomen. Each hair of her coat has a row of tiny spines that help the fur to lie flat and smooth.

TURNING TAIL

The cat's flexible body makes it easy to reach even the most awkward parts of its body.

CATERISTICS

Mutual washing is a sign of affection

No area of the kitten's body is overlooked

Bathtime is part of the daily routine

SLEEPING AND SNOOZING

Adult cats may spend as many as 16 hours in a day sleeping, drifting from deep sleep, through a light doze, to a delicious half-sleep when the eyes may be slightly open. Cats dream, just as humans do, and sleeping cats may purr or twitch their paws during a particularly exciting dream.

WAKING UP

When a cat wakes up from a snooze, he often gives a wide, pink yawn and stretches luxuriously. Then it is time to settle back to sleep, or stand up, give another yawn, and stretch the whole body, arching the back, flexing the front legs and paws, taking a few steps, then stretching the hind legs. Cats behave like this when they want to wake themselves up fully rather than lapsing back into sleep.

Two's Company

For the first few weeks of life, kittens sleep snuggled close together for companionship and warmth. Older cats will behave in exactly the same way, especially if they come from the same litter.

Cateristics

Lots of brief "catnaps" are essential even on the very busiest of days

Tight spaces and narrow ledges are always preferred for a good, long rest

Cats are expert at finding the sunniest spots for a quiet outdoor snooze

Kitten
C A R E

*Everything you need to
know about caring for
your kitten, from
fabulous food to perfect
playtime fun.*

CHOOSING A KITTEN

Choosing a kitten is great fun – but before you decide
there are serious questions to be considered.

WHICH KITTEN?

When you go to choose a kitten, take a good look at the mother as well. If she seems listless or unwell, there's a chance that her kittens will be in poor condition, too. Watch the litter playing together, and go for a kitten with a lively, inquiring nature, who leaps and bounds around with effortless ease. Pick the kitten up and check that eyes are bright, with no sign of the inner eyelid; ears are clean; breath inoffensive, and gums and teeth healthy. Always look through the fur for any signs of fleas. Once you've made your choice, leave your kitten with mom until fully weaned.

EASTERN PROMISE
These tiny Tonkinese kittens will grow up to be intelligent, affectionate companions.

*G*REAT *B*ALLS OF *F*LUFF Longhaired kittens are adorable – but remember that their fine coats will need lots of attention.

*P*EDIGREE OR *N*ON~*P*EDIGREE?
Pedigree kitten or a household cat of character? If the answer is pedigree, go to a known breeder. If you don't want a show cat, breeders may have kittens that are not of "show quality," but make charming pets. Non-pedigree kittens are widely available. Go to an animal charity or watch for advertisements.

*T*HE *L*ONG AND *THE* *S*HORT
Decide if you want a longhaired cat – more unusual than a shorthaired cat, but harder work – or a shorthaired variety that will need little grooming. Do you want a tom or a female? Unneutered toms tend to roam far from home, and may develop anti-social spraying habits. Females, unless neutered, produce regular litters.

TOYS AND GAMES

Kittens love playing games and with these simple
toys, playtime becomes even more exciting.

*F*EATHERLIGHT *F*UN
Hang a feather in a draft so
that it flutters and twirls like
a falling leaf. Kittens find
this lovely for jumping and
pouncing. Have a good supply
of feathers because they don't
survive much tough treatment.

*P*ADDLING *P*OOL
If your feline friend is
fascinated by water,
and a surprising

number of cats are, place a
shallow container of cool water
outside on a hot day and float a
feather or leaf on top. Your cat
will love splashing and dipping
in pursuit of her quarry.

*F*ELINE *F*OOTBALL
*Teach your cat to run, attack,
and score with a ping-pong
ball. Clever puss will
very soon have you
outmaneuvered.*

Cork Punchbag
Attach a length of string to an old wine cork (champagne corks are a good shape) and to a chair back or door frame, so that the cork hangs free for punching practice.

Over the Edge
Place small items – an eraser, a pen, a cotton ball, a toy mouse – between your kitten and the edge of her chair. Out comes the paw, dab, dab, nearer the edge, dab, dab, over it goes. Pick the object up and replace it. Out comes the paw, dab, dab, dab ... Continue until one of you gets weary! (It won't be the kitten.)

Wind Me Up
Give a kitten a small ball of yarn, tightly wound, with one end left tantalizingly loose. Ten minutes later, you have one very happy kitten in a deftly knitted cocoon.

Paper Chase
A discarded newspaper, placed in an inverted "V" on the floor so that it forms an inviting tunnel, will soon sprout legs and start to whirl around the room to the accompaniment of loud ripping noises.

Mouse Pounce
Toy mice, whether they be wind-ups, catnip, or the most basic variety, are always firm favorites with cats.

Essential Equipment

Before you bring your new kitten home, stock up on a few basic items to make her feel welcome. Among the essentials are a warm bed, feeding bowls, a litter box, grooming tools, and a cat carrier. Lots of love and affection are the other vital ingredients.

Ready to Go
A wire cat carrier allows your kitten to study the big, wide world outside, while staying safely confined. Always line the carrier with newspaper and a warm blanket for extra comfort.

Feeding Finesse
By the time they are six to eight weeks old and eating solid foods regularly, kittens should be given individual feeding bowls, which must be thoroughly cleaned before every meal. Place the bowls on sheets of newspaper to avoid messes on the floors.

Eyes Down
Young kittens will share a feeding bowl but when you first bring a kitten home, make sure that she has her own bowl.

Complete Kitten Kit

A brush and comb are all you
need to keep a shorthaired cat
looking smart, although longhairs
may need extra brushes and
combs, as well as taking up more
of your time. Put a collar on your
cat as soon as she starts going out,
though she may object at first.
A name and address tag is
essential in case she should get lost
or wander far from home. A leash
is an optional extra for those cats
who are amenable to training.

Kitten Glamour

Start regular grooming at an early age and your kitten will come to love brush-and-comb sessions. Longhaired kittens need daily grooming to keep their fur free of tangles, but once or twice a week is enough for most shorthaired varieties.

Healthy Claws
Claws rarely need cutting. Ask your vet to show you the best way to trim them safely.

Grooming Guide

1 Begin by brushing the fur upward to remove any trace of tangles and dirt.

2 Comb through gently with a metal comb or slicker brush. Check for signs of fleas.

BRIGHT EYES
Cleanse the eyes
very gently when
necessary, wiping
around the eyes
with a cotton ball
dampened in warm
salt water. Use a clean
piece for each eye.

TOOTH CARE
Remove any build-up of
tartar by brushing gently
with a soft toothbrush and
a salt-water solution.

3 A fine comb will remove
stubborn knots, but take
care not to snag delicate skin.

4 Using a soft toothbrush,
tease out the fur around the
face to create a splendid ruff.

KITTEN CUISINE

Little stomachs need plenty of nourishing and tasty
meals that are easily digested. Here are some
extra-special treats to please your new kitten.
Introduce your kitten to a varied diet right from the
start and you won't have any problems with fussy
eating habits later on. Always allow hot food
to cool to room temperature.

SPECIAL SCRAMBLE

*For two kittens, lightly beat one
egg with a tablespoon of milk.
Scramble the egg gently in a little
melted butter. Place on a dish
to cool, then serve sprinkled
with finely chopped
crisp bacon.*

KITTY BREAKFAST

*For the first meal of the day give
your kitten a small bowl of
cornflakes or baby cereal with
milk. Don't add sugar. Some
cats enjoy a little bowl of
oatmeal, especially on a
cold winter's day.*

Suppertime Treat

Plain cottage cheese mixed with a little flaked salmon (be careful to remove all the bones) makes a delicious, light meal. Try cottage cheese on its own, or with shrimp, for a change.

Savory Snack

Tasty cooking juices from poached fish or braised meat will make a nourishing soup for your kitten. To give substance, add half a slice of crumbled toasted bread to the cooled liquid.

Poacher's Pie

Bake some chicken backs in foil for an hour with water. Remove meat from the bones and chop. Add the cooking liquid. Mix with plain boiled rice.

Toasty Delight

Little squares of toasted bread, spread lightly with cheese spread, will make your kitten's mouth water. Cream cheese or any kind of fish will also be appreciated on cool toast.

Liver Surprise

Simmer chopped chicken livers in stock for 20 minutes until cooked through. Sprinkle with grated cheese and brown under the grill. This scrumptious dish must be cool when served.

Chicken Supreme

For a special treat, offer cooked breast of chicken with a creamy sauce, in a nest of mashed potato. Serve with chopped anchovy on top.

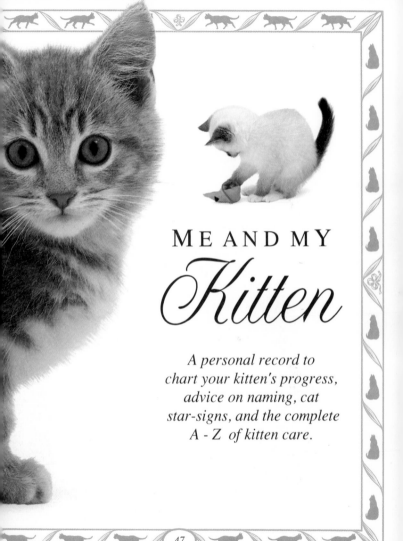

ME AND MY
Kitten

*A personal record to
chart your kitten's progress,
advice on naming, cat
star-signs, and the complete
A - Z of kitten care.*

NAMES AND NAMING

Choosing a name for your kitten is no simple matter. To quote the nineteenth-century author Samuel Butler: "They say that the test of literary power is whether a man can write an inscription. I say, can he name a kitten? And by this test I am condemned, for I cannot." Here are some ideas to set you thinking.

BEATRIX *World-famous English children's writer Beatrix Potter created numerous cats in her books, plump and cuddlesome creatures with wide, innocent eyes.*

BIANCA *The Italian word meaning "white," an appealing name for a fluffy, pure white, female kitten.*

CARRIE CHAPMAN CATT *The American reformer and pacifist who helped secure the vote for women.*

CATALINA *A volcanic island off the coast of Los Angeles.*

CHESHIRE *Inspired by the memorable, smiling Cheshire Cat in the story book* Alice's Adventures in Wonderland *(1865) by Lewis Carroll.*

ELSA *The lioness in* Born Free *by Joy Adamson.*

FIZZY *For a frisky kitten with a champagne personality: lively, bubbly, and never, ever still.*

GALANTHIS *The mythical handmaid who assisted at the birth of Hercules and was transformed by the irate Fates into a cat.*

HOKUSAI *A Japanese artist who painted delicate and detailed cats. Suitable for an elegant, slant-eyed Oriental kitten.*

MAGGIE *The main character in Tennessee Williams's Cat on a Hot Tin Roof. "Nothin's more determined than a cat on a hot tin roof – is there? Is there, baby?"*

PATTIPAWS *One of T. S. Eliot's real cats, who should not be confused with the fictional felines featured in Old Possum's Book of Practical Cats.*

RUMPEL *A nickname given to Samuel Taylor Coleridge's cat. His full name was The Most Noble the Archduke Rumperstilzchen, Marcus Macbum, Earl Tomnefuagne, Baron Raticide, Waowhler, and Scratch, which is rather long for everyday use.*

SEPTIMUS *Literally, it means seventh. A name to use for the last kitten in a large litter. A female kitten could be called Octavia (eighth).*

MY KITTEN'S CALENDAR

❧

Keep a record of your kitten's progress through her first year of life.

My kitten's full name ....

Date of birth ....

Birthplace ....

Sex ....

Color of eyes ....

Color of coat ....

Names of my kitten's parents ....

....

THE FIRST TIME MY KITTEN ...

❧

Meowed ....

Purred ....

Tried solid food ....

Successfully used the litter box ....

Captured a toy mouse ....

Brawled with another kitten ....

Went out of doors ....

Brought home a "catch" ....

Climbed too high and got stuck ....

....

What Makes My Kitten Happy

Favorite foods ....

....

....

Ecstatic stroking spots ....

Coziest corner ....

Sunniest outdoor spot ....

....

Most exciting games ....

....

Cleverest tricks ....

....

KITTEN STARS

Check your kitten's personality in the stars.

ARIES
MARCH 21 – APRIL 20

So full of energy that they never seem to get tired, Arien kittens play, leap, and pounce all day long. They can be very naughty, so teach them "No!" early on. Mothers born under Aries hate to be tied down, and may be off and away once their babies can be left.

TAURUS
APRIL 21 – MAY 21

Bigger than average, these sturdy kittens will constantly be pestering for more milk. They love the security of home and will be slow to venture out on their own. A conscientious Taurean mother dotes on her babies, showering them with love all the time.

GEMINI
MAY 22 – JUNE 21

Full of mischief, these delightful little rascals look as if butter wouldn't melt in their mouths. Geminians are always playful, and keep their kittenish charm through adulthood. Geminian mothers enjoy teaching growing kittens to stalk and pounce.

Cancer
JUNE 22 – JULY 22

Tiny Cancerians are happy youngsters who like heaps of love and affection. Born lap cats, they'll never refuse a cuddle and will follow you around, begging for more. Cancerian mothers are totally devoted, and happiest if none of their kittens leave home.

Leo
JULY 23 – AUGUST 23

A litter of naughty Leos needs to learn discipline from day one, because this sign loves to get its own way. Incurable showoffs, little Leos are great fun to watch. Leo mothers give their kittens lots of freedom, but make sure they know *just* how far to go.

Virgo
AUGUST 24 – SEPTEMBER 22

Bright as buttons, young Virgoans show their intelligence right from the word go. They can be rather nervous and are easily frightened if strangers try to handle them. A Virgoan mother is very patient; nothing is too much trouble when it comes to kitten care.

LIBRA
SEPTEMBER 23 – OCTOBER 23

These babies like to spend as much time as possible curled up together, fast asleep. When they are not snoozing, Libran kittens are content to spend hours lazily grooming. Libran mothers never have favorites; each kitten receives equal love and attention.

SCORPIO
OCTOBER 24 – NOVEMBER 22

Every kitten in a Scorpio litter wants to be the center of attention, all the time. This can lead to hissing and even fisticuffs, although no one ever gets hurt. A Scorpio mother is a real tigress who will fight tooth and claw if her kittens are threatened.

SAGITTARIUS
NOVEMBER 23 – DECEMBER 21

Young Sagittarians whirl through the house like tiny hurricanes, running up the curtains, twirling around after their tails, and leaping on each other from great heights. Sagittarian mothers, forever young at heart, join in the kitten play when no one's looking!

CAPRICORN
DECEMBER 22 – JANUARY 20

Capricornians have a serious streak even as kittens. They love learning, and poke their noses in everywhere, so that they can find out more about their fascinating world. A Capricornian mother hates watching her babies struggle and always rushes in to help.

AQUARIUS
JANUARY 21 – FEBRUARY 18

These little rebels can be decidedly wayward and don't respond well to the voice of authority. This sign never wants to conform and is always strongly individual. Aquarian mothers encourage their kittens to develop their own personalities right from the start.

PISCES
FEBRUARY 19 – MARCH 20

Angelic Piscean kittens positively invite you to spoil them, and you'll find this hard to resist. Don't fall into their trap, because you'll have to pamper them for life. Piscean mothers are very protective, always anxious to shield their young from the dangers of the world.

A-Z OF KITTEN CARE

A IS FOR
AILMENTS
If your kitten
develops a tickly
cough or runny
nose, loses appetite
or appears listless,
ask the vet to have
a look at her.

B IS FOR BUYING
Steer clear of pet
shops. One of the
animal protection
societies will be
glad to supply a
kitten or, for a
pedigree, go to a
known breeder.

C IS FOR CUDDLES
Handle kittens with
care and avoid
squeezing delicate
little bodies too
hard. Never pick a
kitten up by the
scruff of the neck or
by the "armpits" –
support the rear
end as well.

D IS FOR DANGER
Keep kittens out of
the kitchen and
away from sources
of direct heat.
Beware of tiny toys
and objects which
could choke. Keep
washers and dryers,
refrigerators,
freezers, and ovens
firmly closed.

E IS FOR EARS
Clean dirt or wax
away very gently
with moistened
cotton swabs.

F IS FOR FEEDING
Increase the
amount of food you
give as your kitten
grows. Don't worry
about overfeeding –
cats stop eating
when they've had
enough. Give three
small meals a day
up to five months,
then feed larger
meals twice daily.

G IS FOR
GREENERY
Kittens love to
nibble houseplants
– keep them out of
reach. Remember
that it is quite
natural for cats to
eat grass.

H IS FOR
HOUSE-TRAINING
Start early, at three
weeks, popping a
kitty into the litter
box after meals.

I IS FOR
INDEPENDENCE
Babyhood is soon
over. By ten weeks
a kitten is eating
solids and is ready
to explore the big,
wide world.

J IS FOR JUMPING
By six weeks, a
kitten can run and
jump, although it
may sometimes
misjudge a distance.

K IS FOR KITTENS
If you don't want
more kittens than
you bargained for,
have your young cat
neutered when
she's between four
and six months old.

L IS FOR LEAVING
When six months
old, kittens can be
left for up to 24
hours, if food and
water are provided.

M IS FOR MICE
And birds, flies, or
any other
unsuspecting
creature your kitten
catches. Some cats
are born hunters,
and unfortunately
there's very little
you can do to curb
their natures.

N IS FOR
NIGHTTIME
Never allow a
kitten, or cat, to
stay out all night.
That's when most
road accidents
happen, and cat
thieves prowl. The
safest place for your
kitten is warmly
tucked up in his
very own bed.

O IS FOR YOUR
OTHER PETS
Dogs, and even
other cats, can
learn to tolerate,
and love, kittens.
Introduce new
members of the
household gradually
and allow plenty of
time for adjustment
to achieve the
happiest results.

P IS FOR PEDIGREE
If you think you
might want to show
your cat, make sure
that the complete
pedigree and any
change of address
and ownership are
registered with a
cat registry at five
weeks of age.

Q IS FOR QUEEN

Giving birth to a large litter of kittens can be exhausting for a queen, and she will need to rest for 12 to 24 hours. By the second day she should be getting back to normal. The queen bonds with her litter by rubbing their heads with her own to transfer scent. During the first three months of her kittens' lives she will teach them all they need to know. Never separate mother and kitten until the kitten is fully weaned.

R IS FOR REARING

Kittens may be reared by hand if, for some reason, their mother cannot raise them. They need to be kept at a constant, warm temperature and to be fed with a bottle, or, if they are very reluctant feeders, with a dropper. The process requires time and patience. A vet can advise on formulas and feeding methods.

S IS FOR SCRATCHING

A kitten who starts scratching furiously may have picked up fleas. Treat with a spray or powder from your vet.

T IS FOR TRAVEL

From time to time you will need to transport your kitten. Cardboard carriers are available, but won't resist a determined attempt to escape. A carrying case with a see-through plastic cover is best for use on public transportation. A mesh basket made of plastic and lined with a blanket for warmth is long lasting, washable, and easy to secure. Any container needs a newspaper lining in case of mishaps *en route* and a blanket for comfort. Never leave your cat in a carrier alone in a car because temperatures in enclosed spaces can rise rapidly in hot weather, causing great distress.

U IS FOR UPSIDE-DOWN

When your kitten rolls over and invites you to stroke her fluffy abdomen, she is remembering the delightful sensation of having her underside groomed by her mother. Watch out as this is also a favorite fighting position.

V IS FOR VACCINATIONS

Vital for your kitten's health. Make sure your kitten is vaccinated against feline enteritis and influenza a minimum of seven days before taking her home. Annual boosters are essential if you ever intend to put your kitten into a boarding cattery.

W IS FOR WEANING

At around four weeks, a kitten's diet of milk can be supplemented with solid food. By eight weeks the kitten will be eating solids at every meal, and be fully weaned.

X IS FOR XERCISE

Never a problem with kittens, who race around all day, pausing only to collapse in an exhausted heap before the next explosion of energy. Kittens soon lose their youthful exuberance and become more sedate. Adult cats may sleep for 12 to 16 hours per day.

Y IS FOR YOWLING

The unmistakable sound produced by amorous cats. Unneutered females can mate at around six months to a year, but males are not mature enough until 12 to 15 months old. Kittens learn to make sounds over a period of months, and may not give a full-blooded "meow" until they are fairly grown up.

Z IS FOR ZODIAC

Discover the true character of your kitten in the stars; *see* Kitten Stars on pages 52–55.

I N D E X

ACKNOWLEDGMENTS

*All photography by Jane Burton except for:
Steve Shott: page 19 (bottom left)*

Design Assistance: *Patrizio Semproni, Ursula Dawson, Camilla Fox*
Illustrations: *Susan Robertson, Stephen Lings, Clive Spong*

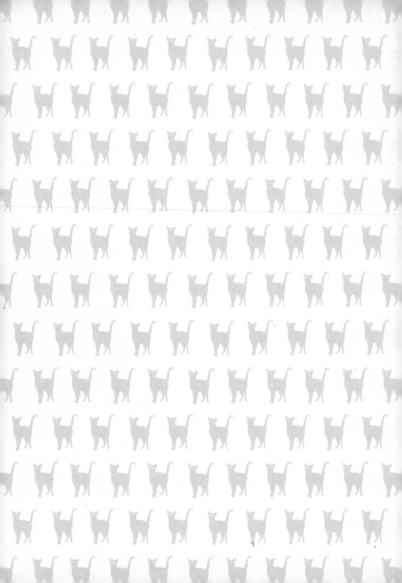